CU00686777

With Thanks

Elizabeth Rundle

HUNT&
THORPE

Copyright © 1994 Hunt & Thorpe
Text © 1994 E Rundle
Cover illustration © Sue Climpson

ISBN 1 85608 141 9

In Australia this book is published by:
Hunt & Thorpe Australia Pty Ltd.
9 Euston Street, Rydalmere NSW 2116

A CIP catalogue record for this book is available
from the British Library

Manufactured in Singapore

INTRODUCTION

'Ingratitude – thou marble-hearted fiend' goes the saying. And we all heartily agree! Soft hearts can say, 'sorry', and 'thank you' too. But sometimes a simple word is not enough. How can we fully express the gratitude we feel? And there are so many things one can say 'thank you' for – a thoughtful word, a meal, a holiday, help with a prob-lem, a letter, a gift, time simply spent in listening. This book helps us convey sincere, warm, deep thanks for something simple or very profound.

*The greatest blessing
is a pleasant friend.*

HORACE, 65-8BC

No one is rich enough to be without friends. Make new friends but keep the old. New are silver; old are gold.

AUTHOR UNKNOWN

*So long as we love, we serve so
long as we are loved by others
I would almost say that we are
indispensable; and no man is
useless while he has a friend.*

ROBERT LOUIS STEVENSON,
1850-1894

*Love makes
everything lovely.*

GEORGE MACDONALD,
1824-1905

Christianity has taught us to care.

Caring is the greatest thing.

Caring matters most.

Friedrich von Hugel,
Letters from Baron Hugel to his niece

By this all men will know that
you are my disciples,
if you love one another.

THE BIBLE, JESUS CHRIST,
JOHN 13:35

God does not comfort us
to make us comfortable,
but to make us comforters.

J.H. JOWETT,
1864-1923

Life has no pleasure higher or nobler than that of friendship.

SAMUEL JOHNSON,
1709-1784

*He touched nothing
that he did not adorn.*

EPITAPH FOR OLIVER GOLDSMITH,
1728-1774

The more we love, the better we are, and the greater our friendships are, the dearer we are to God.

JEREMY TAYLOR,
1613-1667

Good deeds that are done silently
and for a good motive, are the dead
that live even in the grave; they are
the flowers that withstand the
storm; they are the stars that
know no setting.

CLAUDIUS,
10BC-AD54

Though we do not have our Lord with us in bodily presence, we have our neighbour, who, for the ends of love and loving service, is as good as our Lord himself.

TERESA OF AVILA,
1515-1582

And so the shadows fall apart,
And so the west winds play;
And all the windows of my heart
I open to the day

JOHN GREENLEAF WHITTIER
1807-1892

He who kisses the joy as it flies

Lives in eternity's sunrise.

WILLIAM BLAKE,
1757-1827

*For God did not give us a spirit
of timidity, but a spirit of power,
of love and of self-control.*

THE BIBLE, THE APOSTLE PAUL,
2 TIMOTHY 1:7

*God's gifts put man's best
dreams to shame.*

ELIZABETH BARRETT BROWNING,
1806-1861

My God, how wonderful Thou art,
Thy majesty how bright!
How beautiful Thy mercy-seat,
In depths of burning light!

F.W. FABER,
1814-1863

Of courtesy it is much less
Than courage of heart or holiness,
Yet in my walks it seems to me
That the grace of God is
in courtesy.

HILAIRE BELLOC,
1870-1953

For the beauty of the earth,
For the beauty of the skies,
For the love which from our birth
Over and around us lies:
Father, unto thee we raise
This our sacrifice of praise.

F.S. PIERPOINT,
1835-1917

Those who possess good friends

are truly rich.

SPANISH PROVERB

True greatness consists
in being great in little things.

DR JOHNSON, 1709-1784

Kindness is a language the blind

can see and the deaf can hear.

AUTHOR UNKNOWN

We always thank God for all of you, mentioning you in our prayers.

THE BIBLE, THE APOSTLE PAUL,
1 THESSALONIANS 1:2

To us what matters is an individual.

MOTHER TERESA OF CALCUTTA,
BORN 1910

*The person who has
stopped being thankful has fallen
asleep in life.*

ROBERT LOUIS STEVENSON,
1850-1894

*The best way to cheer yourself
is to try to cheer somebody else up.*

MARK TWAIN,
1835-1910

Beauty is God's handwriting.
Welcome it in every fair face,
every fair day, every fair flower.

CHARLES KINGSLEY,
1819-1875

*A faithful friend is
an image of God.*

FRENCH PROVERB

O God, we thank you for this earth, our home; for the wide sky and the blessed sun, for the salt sea and the running water,...

...for the everlasting hills and the
never-resting winds, for trees and
the common grass underfoot.

WALTER RAUSCHENBUSCH,
1861-1916

I will praise you, O Lord,

with all my heart;

I will tell of you wonders.

THE BIBLE,
PSALM 9:1

Give thanks in all circumstances,
for this is God's will for you...

☽

THE BIBLE, THE APOSTLE PAUL,
1 THESSALONIANS 5:18

Now thank we all our God
With heart and hand and voices,
Who wondrous things hath done,
In whom his world rejoices...

... Who from our mother's arms
Hath blessed us on our way
With countless gifts of love,
And still is our today.

M RINKART, 1586-1649,
TRANSLATED C. WINKWORTH

These have I loved...
Wet roofs, beneath the lamp-light;
the strong crust Of friendly bread;
and many tasting food;
Rainbows and the blue bitter
smoke of wood...

☾

RUPERT BROOKE,
1887-1915

A thing of beauty is a joy for ever:

Its loveliness increases; it will never

Pass into nothingness...

JOHN KEATS,
1795-1821

...but still will keep

A bower of quiet for us, and a sleep

Full of sweet dreams, and health

and quiet breathing.

JOHN KEATS,

1795-1821

A judicious friend, into whose bosom we may pour out our souls, and tell our corruptions as well as our comforts, is a great privilege.

GEORGE WHITFIELD,
1714-1770

There is no duty we so much
underrate as the duty of being
happy. By being happy we sow
anonymous benefits upon
the world.

R.L. STEVENSON,
1850-1894

If a man be gracious to strangers
it shows that he is a citizen of the
world and that his heart is no
island, cut off from other islands,
but a continent that joins them.

FRANCIS BACON,
1561-1626

If I can ease one life the aching,

Or cool one pain,

Or help one fainting robin

Unto his nest again

I shall not live in vain.

EMILY DICKENSON,
1830-1886

Let all the world

in every corner sing,

My God and King!

GEORGE HERBERT,
1593-1633

Love is something more stern and splendid than mere kindness.

C.S. Lewis,
1898-1963

When I stop praying the coincidences stop happening.

WILLIAM TEMPLE,
1881-1944

If our love were but more simple,
We should take him at his word
And our lives would be all sunshine
In the sweetness of our Lord.

⪼⪢◦⪡⪻

F.W. Faber,
1814-1863

I have experienced that the habit of taking out of the hand of our Lord every little blessing and brightness on our path, confirms us, in an especial manner, in communion with his love.

M.A. SCHIMMELENINCK

What inexpressible joy for me, to
look up through the apple-blossom
and the fluttering leaves, and to
see God's love there...

...to know that if I could unwrap
fold after fold of God's universe,
I should only unfold more and
more blessing and see deeper and
deeper into the love which is at the
heart of it all.

ELIZABETH CHARLES,
BORN ABOUT 1826

Friendship is a golden chain …

Time can't destroy its beauty

For, as long as memory lives

Years can't erase the pleasure

That the joy of friendship gives.

HELEN STEINER RICE

THANKS   51

*The one who will be found in trial
capable of great acts of love, is ever
the one who is doing considerate
small ones.*

F.W. ROBERTSON

What lovely things
Thy hand hath made;
The smooth-plumed bird
In its emerald shade...

...The seed of grass,
The speck of stone
Which the wayfaring ant
Stirs – and hastes on!

WALTER DE LA MARE,
1873-1956

Into all our lives, in many simple, familiar, homely ways, God infuses this element of joy from the surprises of life...

...*the strain of music...or sunset glory...the unsought word of encouragement...these are the overflowing riches of His grace, these are his free gifts.*

S. LONGFELLOW,
1819-1892

I do not agree with the big way of doing things. To us what matters is an individual. To get to love the person we must come in close contact with him.

MOTHER TERESA OF CALCUTTA,
BORN 1910

*The really great man is the man
who makes every man feel great.*

G.K. CHESTERTON,
1874-1936

Let us, with a gladsome mind,

Praise the Lord, for he is kind:

For his mercies ay endure,

Ever faithful, ever sure.

JOHN MILTON,
1608-1674

The more we love, the better we are, and the greater our friendships are, the dearer we are to God.

JEREMY TAYLOR,
1613-1667

Life goes headlong...
But if suddenly we encounter a
friend, we pause.

R.W. EMERSON,
1803-1882

To see eternity in a grain of sand

And heaven in a wild flower,

Hold infinity in the palm

of your hand

And eternity in an hour.

WILLIAM BLAKE,
1757-1827

Better is open rebuke than hidden love. Wounds from a friend can be trusted, but an enemy multiplies kisses.

THE BIBLE,
PROVERBS 27:5-6

Iron sharpeneth iron; so a man sharpeneth the countenance of his friend.

THE BIBLE,
PROVERBS 27:17, AV

The best way of knowing God is to frequent the company of his friends.

ST TERESA,
1515-1582

*P*raise the Lord.

How good it is to sing praises

to our God.

THE BIBLE,
PSALM 147:1

A saint is one who makes it easy to believe in Jesus.

RUTH GRAHAM BELL

Look thy last on all things lovely,
Every hour — let no night
Seal thy sense in deathly slumber
Till to delight
Thou hast paid thy utmost
blessing.

WALTER DE LA MARE,
1873-1956

Expect great things from God.

Attempt great things for God.

MOTTO OF MISSIONARY
WILLIAM CAREY, 1761-1834

A man of many companions may come to ruin, but there is a friend who sticks closer than a brother.

THE BIBLE,
PROVERBS 18:24

It [friendship] redoubleth joys,
and cutteth griefs in halves.

FRANCIS BACON,
1561-1626

Blessed are those whose strength is in you [God] who have set their hearts on pilgrimage. ...They go from strength to strength.

THE BIBLE,
PSALM 84:5,7

Have you had a kindness shown?

Pass it on!

'Twas not given for thee alone,

Pass it on...

...*Let it travel down the years,*

Let it wipe another's tears,

Till in heaven the deed appears –

Pass it on!

HENRY BURTON,
c.1886

Earth's crammed with heaven
And every common bush afire with
God: But only he who sees takes
off his shoes – The rest sit round it
and pluck blackberries.

ELIZABETH BARRETT BROWNING,
1806-1861

When all thy mercies,

O my God,

My rising soul surveys,

Transported with the view I'm lost

In wonder, love and praise.

JOSEPH ADDISON,
1672-1719

*Jonathan loved David as much
as he loved himself.*

THE BIBLE,
1 SAMUEL 20:17

No one is useless in this world
who lightens the burden of another.

CHARLES DICKENS,
1812-1870

Give thanks to the Lord for his unfailing love and his wonderful deeds for men, for he satisfies the thirsty, and fills the hungry with good things.

THE BIBLE,
PSALM 107:8,9

The angels keep their ancient places – Turn but a stone, and start a wing! Tis we, tis our estranged faces That miss the many-splendoured thing.

FRANCIS THOMPSON,
1859-1907

To get the best out of life great

matters have to be given

a second thought.

PLAISE PASCAL,
1623-1662

To my God a heart of flame
To my fellow-men a heart of love;
To myself a heart of steel.

AUGUSTINE,
354-430

Do not waste time bothering about whether you love your neighbour; act as if you did... When you are behaving as if you love someone, you will presently come to love him.

C.S. LEWIS,
1898-1963

The way from God to a human heart is through a human heart.

S.D GORDON

My heart is like a singing bird,
Whose nest is in a watered shoot;
My heart is like an apple-tree
Whose boughs are bent with
thickest fruit.

CHRISTINA ROSSETTI,
1830-1894

*And they who fain
would serve Thee best
Are conscious most of
wrong within.*

H. TWELLS,
1823-1900

Love is without doubt the
strongest force in the universe.

AUTHOR UNKNOWN